D0899024

MY FIRST SKETCHBOOK

# DRAWING
# VEHICLES
## A Step-by-Step Sketchbook

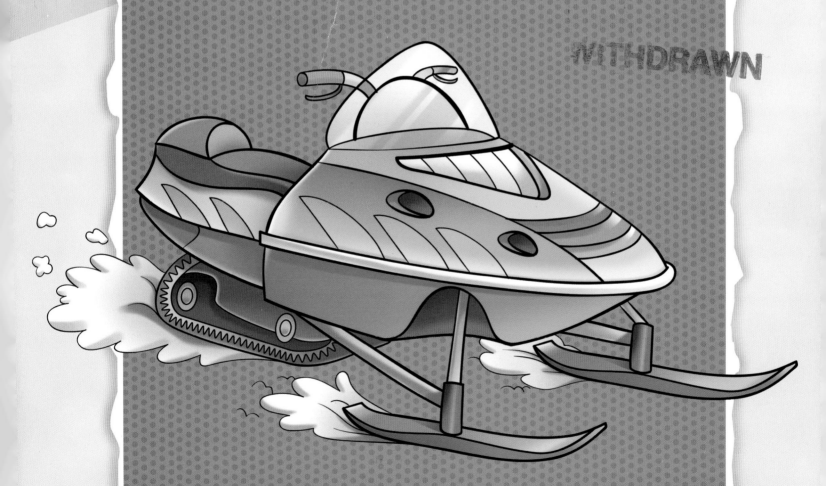

by Mari Bolte
illustrated by Lucy Makuc

CAPSTONE PRESS
a capstone imprint

First Facts are published by Capstone Press,
1710 Roe Crest Drive, North Mankato, Minnesota 56003
www.capstonepub.com

**Library of Congress Cataloging-in-Publication Data**
Bolte, Mari, author.
  Drawing vehicles : a step-by-step sketchbook / by Mari Bolte ; illustrated by Lucy Makuc.
      pages cm. — (First facts. My first sketchbook)
  Summary: "Step-by-step instructions and sketches show how to draw a variety of
vehicles"—Provided by publisher.
  ISBN 978-1-4914-0283-2 (library binding)
  ISBN  978-1-4914-0288-7 (eBook PDF)
1.  Vehicles in art—Juvenile literature. 2.  Drawing—Technique—Juvenile literature.  I.
Makuc, Lucy, illustrator. II. Title.
  NC825.V45B65 2015
  743.89629046--dc23                                          2014013817

**Editorial Credits**
Juliette Peters, designer; Katy LaVigne, production specialist


**Photo Credits**
Capstone Studio: Karon Dubke, 5 (photos); Shutterstock: Azuzl (design element), Kalenik
Hannah (design element), oculo (design element)

Printed in the United States of America in North Mankato, Minnesota.
052014      008087CGF14

# TABLE of CONTENTS

# SPEEDY SKETCHES

Trains, trucks, and planes,
and cars that go, "Vroom!"
Sketching vehicles is fun,
and learning to draw is too!

Rev your engines and get ready to draw! Follow these tips and the simple steps on each page. You'll be drawing powerful, fast, and high-flying vehicles in no time.

**TIP 1** **Draw lightly.** You will need to erase some lines as you go, so draw them light.

**TIP 2** **Add details.** Little details, such as headlights or exhaust clouds, make your drawings more realistic.

**TIP 3** **Color your drawings.** Color can make a flat drawing jump off the page!

You won't need a propeller or gasoline.
But you will need some supplies.

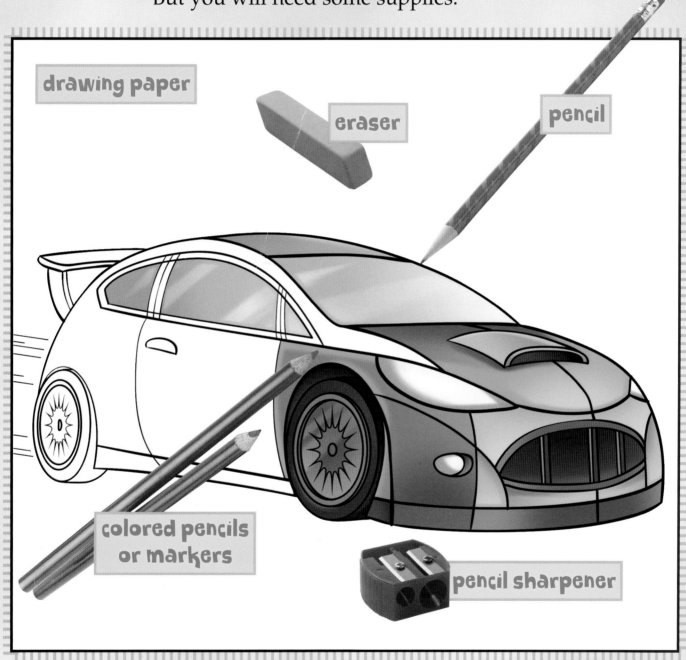

drawing paper

eraser

pencil

colored pencils
or markers

pencil sharpener

Sharpen your pencils, and get ready to draw
vehicles on the road, in the water, and through the sky.
Soon you'll be sketching at full speed!

# STREAMING JET

Get ready for takeoff! The speediest jets can fly faster than 1,500 miles (2,414 kilometers) per hour. Can you keep up?

Final

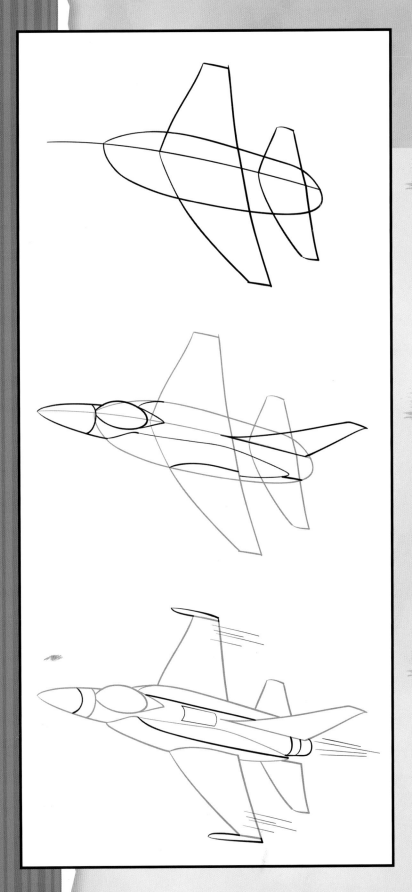

Draw a slightly curved line.
Add an oval shape around the
line. Draw two triangles with
squared ends for wings.

Draw a half triangle with squared
ends for the tail. Add a cone shape
for the jet's nose and an oval
behind the cone for a window.
Add detail lines on the jet's
window, nose, and wings.

Draw two thicker lines along the
jet's back. Add two long, thin ovals
to the ends of the larger wings.
Sketch detail lines for the jet's
exhaust and to add motion.

# MONSTER TRUCK

Monster trucks don't go around—they go over and through! Draw this king of the road doing what it does best.

Final

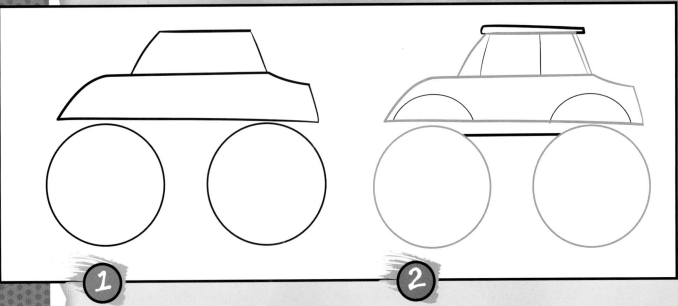

**1**

Draw two large circles for tires. Draw an upside-down boat shape over the circles. Add a rectangle on top.

**2**

Add a line to connect the two tires. Draw a thin rectangle on top of the truck and two half-circles on the bottom. Sketch detail lines for the truck's windows.

**3**

Add a long, thin rectangle under the trucks's body, and another line between the tires. Draw more detail lines for the truck's door. Add small circles inside the tires.

**4**

Sketch detail lines for the truck's headlight, back hatch, and suspension arms. Add circles slightly larger than the circles you drew in Step 3 for the inside of the tires.

# RED RESCUER

Everyone recognizes a fire engine! Put out the fire by drawing this helpful truck in action.

Final

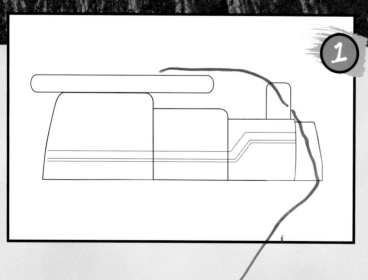

**1** Draw three squares. Each square should be a little smaller than the last. Sketch a long zig-zag line through all the squares. Draw a flat rectangle on top of the first square. Add two tall rectangles on the top and side of the third square.

**2**

Draw a tilted rectangle to connect the flat
and tall rectangle on the top of the truck.
Add a tall rectangle inside the first square.
Add a square inside the center square. Then
add half-circles for tires. Sketch detail lines
under the zig-zag line and inside the end
rectangle. Add a few more detail lines for
the truck's headlight and bumper.

**3**

Add detail lines inside every
square and rectangle drawn in
Step 2 (except the tilted rectangle.)
Add circles for tires and squares
or rectangles for windows. Use
small squares and detail lines to
draw the siren lights.

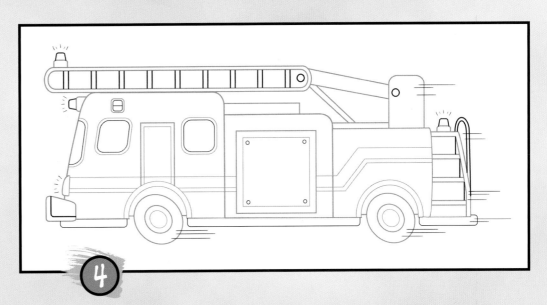

**4**

Sketch detail lines inside the top rectangle for the
ladder. Add a curved line to the end rectangle for
a railing. Additional detail lines will finish your
fire truck and give it movement.

# TREASURE HUNTER

Whether it's hauling up fish or scooping
up buried treasure, this boat can do it all!

Draw a V shape with two curved lines.
One line should be longer than the
other. Add a curving line that connects
the ends of the V. Add another curved
line across the top for the edge of the
boat. Sketch detail lines along the top
and front of the boat.

Draw a cube shape on top of the
boat. Add a smaller cube behind
it. Draw a circle and curved lines
for the life preserver. Draw a small
circle on the back of the boat. Add
more detail lines along the top and
front of the boat.

Draw a long, thin, pointy triangle
near the back of the boat. Add a
circle at the top and a larger circle
at the base, for a winch. Add two
more pointy triangles to the front
of the cube. Add a small rectangle
with rounded corners for a window
and a detail line around the cube.

**4**

Add curved lines for a hook and straight lines for a net. Add detail lines around the side of the boat and at the base of the winch. Draw a circle for a side window.

**5**

Draw scalloped lines for the rest of the net. Add detail lines to the round window.

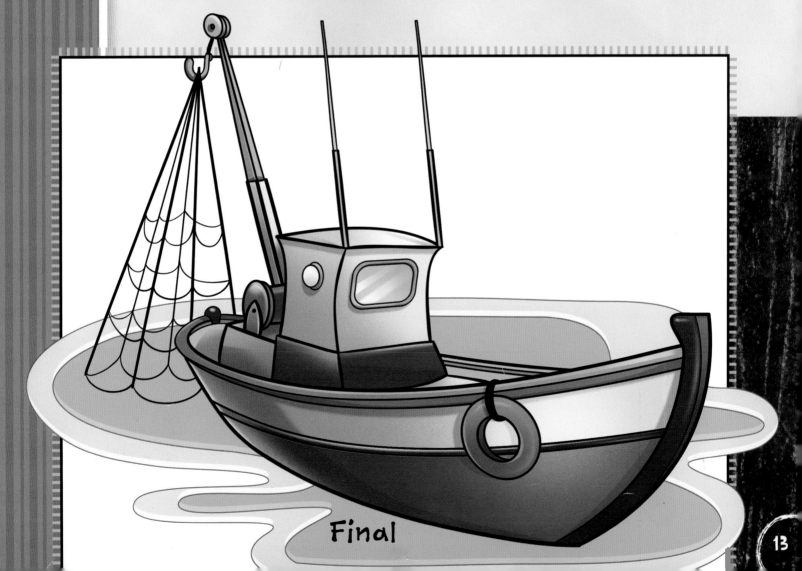

Final

# AIR RESCUE

Whether you're going from one hospital to another, or coming from a remote location, this sky-high speeder will get you to safety in no time.

Final

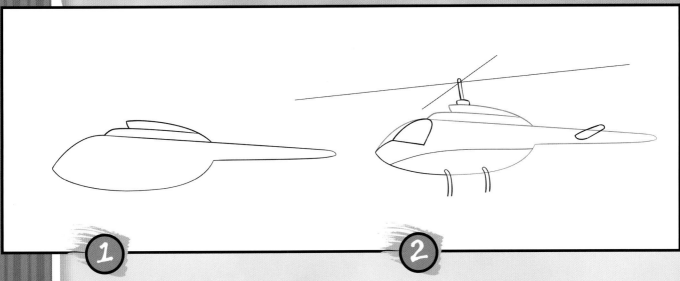

**1**

Draw a tadpole shape. Use curved and straight lines to add detail to the top of the helicopter.

**2**

Add a small square and tall rectangle to the top. Sketch two long lines that criss-cross over the tall rectangle. Add an oval shape on the tail. Use curved lines to start landing skids.

**3**

Add two more long lines for the helicopter's propeller blades. Draw squares on the helicopter's body. Use curved lines to add a tail. Add a long, curved line beneath the helicopter. Don't forget to add more lines for the landing skids on the right side.

**4**

Add another long, curved line beneath the helicopter. Draw two small squares for windows. Then draw a plus sign in the small square from Step 3. Add a small tail propeller. Then use detail lines around the propellers to show that the helicopter is in flight.

# TOUGH TANK

Tanks are armored vehicles designed to defend and attack. A tank's coloring helps keep it hidden. Its caterpillar tracks help it defeat any terrain. What's your strategy for drawing this tough tank?

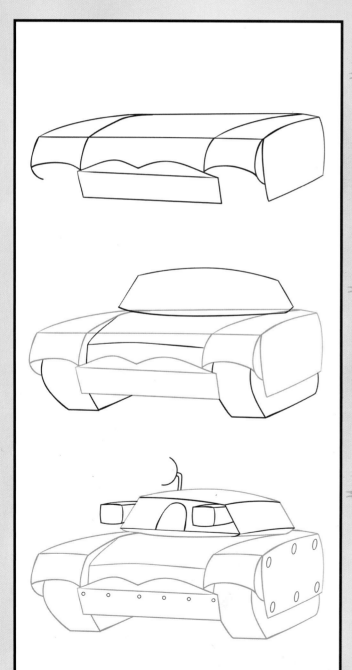

 **1**

Draw a large rectangular shape with curved corners. Give the bottom of the rectangle scalloped lines. Add a smaller rectangle below the scallops. Use detail lines to give the large rectangle more curves.

 **2**

Use curved and straight lines to add a dome shape to the top of the tank. Use more lines to add caterpillar tracks. Add a detail line along the middle of the large rectangle.

 **3**

Use curved and straight lines to add detail to the top of the tank. Add small circles along the front and sides of the tank.

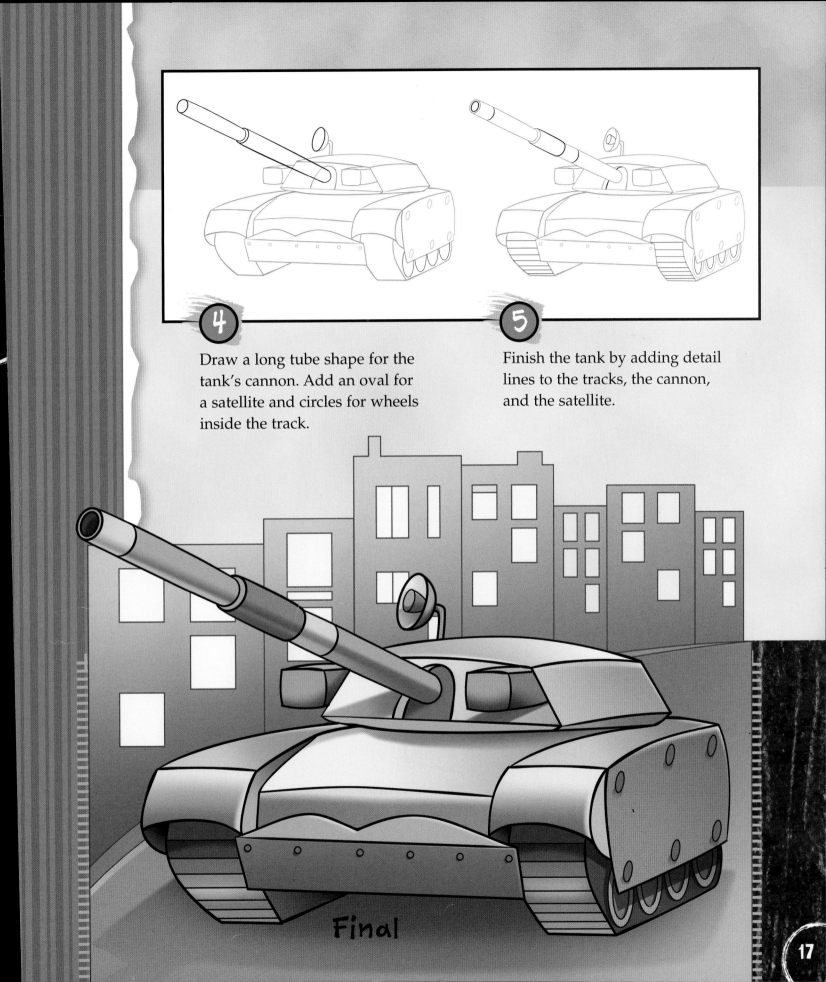

**4**

Draw a long tube shape for the tank's cannon. Add an oval for a satellite and circles for wheels inside the track.

**5**

Finish the tank by adding detail lines to the tracks, the cannon, and the satellite.

Final

# BULLET TRAIN

Bullet trains are super speedy vehicles passengers can ride on to get from one place to another. Traveling at speeds of more than 300 miles (483 kilometers) per hour, this train might soar right off the page!

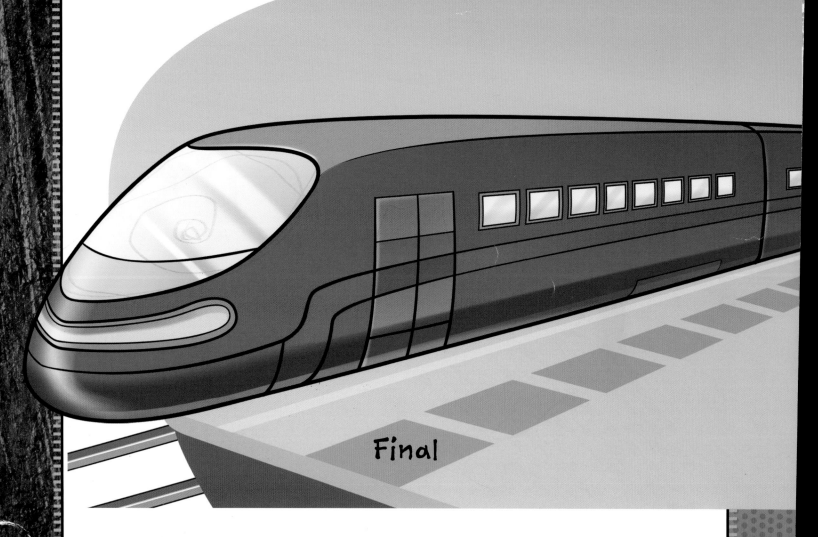

Final

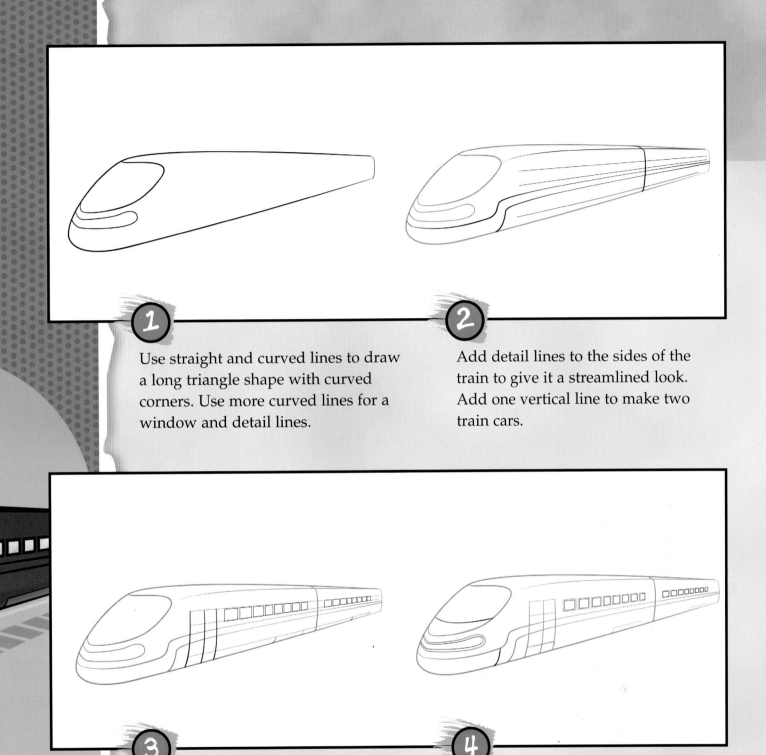

**1** Use straight and curved lines to draw a long triangle shape with curved corners. Use more curved lines for a window and detail lines.

**2** Add detail lines to the sides of the train to give it a streamlined look. Add one vertical line to make two train cars.

**3** Add two rectangles for doors. Draw small squares for windows.

**4** Draw detail lines around the front of the train and around each window.

# RALLY RACER

Rally cars race on many types of roads and in many kinds of conditions. Whether it's going through the dirt, in the snow, or on a regular road, a rally car will get you where you need to go.

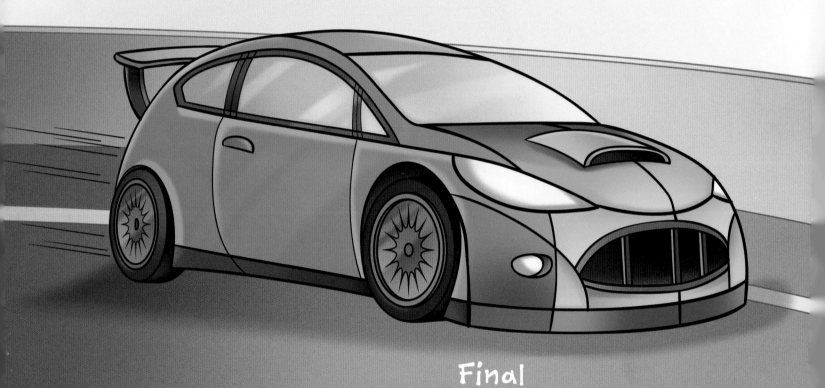

Final

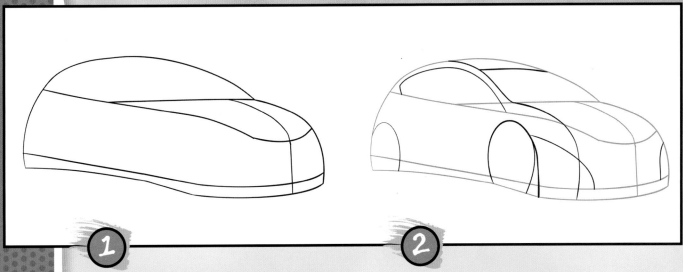

**①** Use straight and curved lines to draw a general car shape. Use a curved line to outline the car's hood.

**②** Draw two circles for wheels. Add curved lines to add more detail to the car's hood, windshield, and windows.

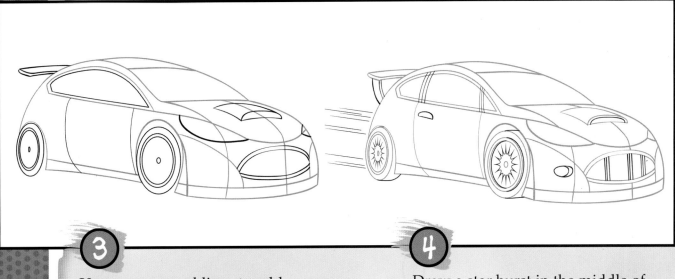

**③** Use more curved lines to add headlights, a grille, and a hood scoop to the front of the car. Draw smaller circles inside the tires and the side window. Add a rectangle shape for the car's spoiler. Use curved lines for a door.

**④** Draw a star burst in the middle of both tires. Use detail lines to add window details, a door handle, and fog lights. Add curved lines to connect the spoiler to the car. Then draw motion lines.

# SNOW SPEEDER

Snowmobiles get you from here to there in the coldest of seasons. Draw this snow speeder skating over the steepest drifts.

Final

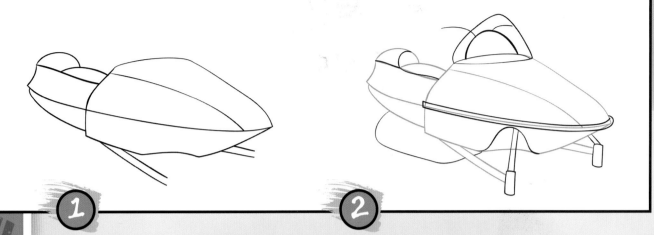

**1**

Use straight and curved lines to draw the body of the snowmobile. Add four straight lines underneath.

**2**

Add more straight lines that connect to the straight lines in Step 1. Draw a curved line underneath for the track. Add a triangle shape for the windshield and curved lines for the dashboard and handlebars. Add curved lines for detail to the front of the snowmobile.

**3**

Draw long smile shapes for the skis. Add a triangle for the headlights. Use detail lines to add vents, handles, and the bottom of the seat. Add a curved line and small circles on the track. Sketch scalloped lines for flying snow.

**4**

Add shark fin shapes along the entire snowmobile for decoration. Draw detail lines along the track and headlights. Make sure both handles have brakes. Then let the snow fly!

# READ MORE

**Cerato, Mattia**. *Easy to Draw Vehicles*. You Can Draw. Mankato, Minn.: Picture Window Books, 2012.

**Kissock, Heather**. *Military Vehicles*. Learn to Draw. New York: AV2 by Weigl, 2013.

**Porter, Steve**. *Sports Cars*. You Can Draw It! Minneapolis: Bellwether Media, Inc., 2014.

# INTERNET SITES

FactHound offers a safe, fun way to find Internet sites related to this book. All of the sites on FactHound have been researched by our staff.

www.FactHound.com

Here's all you do:

Visit *www.facthound.com*

Type in this code: 9781491402832

Super-cool stuff!

Check out projects, games and lots more at **www.capstonekids.com**